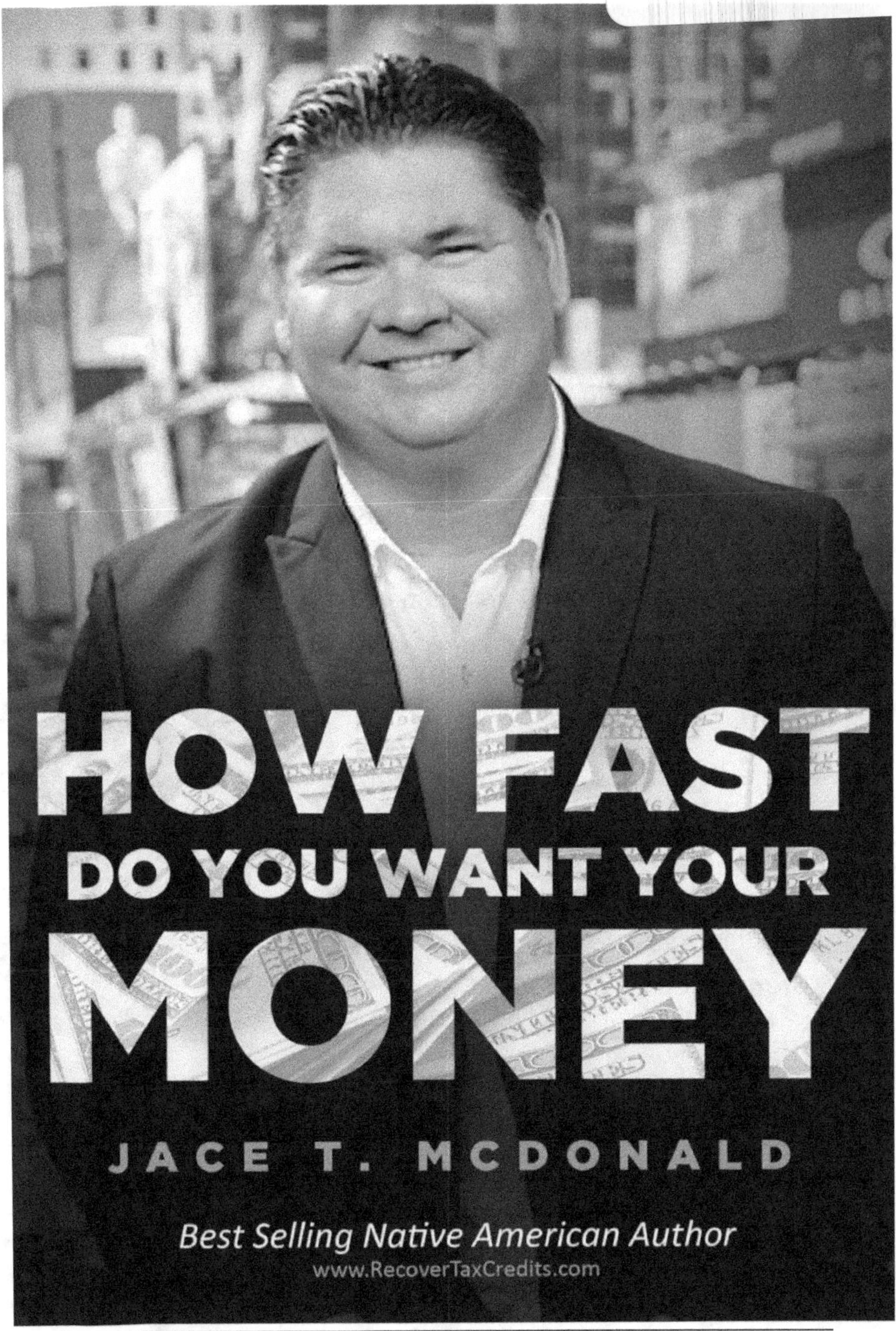
HOW FAST
DO YOU WANT YOUR
MONEY
JACE T. MCDONALD
Best Selling Native American Author
www.RecoverTaxCredits.com

How Fast Do You Want Your Money?

Business owners are missing out on tax credits, tax incentives, and tax savings. As a small business owner, these could make the difference between your survival or demise during these tough times. This is not just for big business. We not only help business owners, but baby boomers, retirees, and people who want to retire someday.

*We didn't plan to be tax credit experts; we fell into this via a series of accidents. We are blessed we have solutions that will forever change your financial outcome and that of your children and your children's children. Please keep an open mind as you learn of this privileged information,
most have never heard of many of the things mentioned in this book.*

Jace T. McDonald

How Fast Do You Want Your Money?

Trademark ™ 2020 by Driving Force Company LLC

All rights reserved. Copyright under Berne Copyright Convention, Universal Copyright Convention, and Pan-American Copyright Convention. No part of this book may be reproduced, stored in a retrieval system, or transmitted in any form, or by any means, electronic, mechanical, photocopying, recording or otherwise, without prior permission of the author.

ISBN: 9798628770115

Published by Driving Force Company LLC

Disclaimer

While the authors have used their best efforts in preparing this book, they make no representations or warranties with respect to accuracy or completeness of the contents of this book. The advice and strategies contained herein may not be suitable for your situation. You should consult a professional where appropriate. The authors shall not be liable for any loss of profit or any other special, incidental, consequential, or other damages. The purchaser or reader of this publication assumes responsibility for the use of these materials and information. Adherence to all applicable laws and regulations, both advertising and all other aspects of doing business in the United States or any other jurisdiction, is the sole responsibility of the purchaser or reader.

Need Help To Get Your Money Back That You've Overpaid?

Go to:
www.RecoverTaxCredits.com

Preface

As you read this book remember, as a young man I employed hundreds of people at a construction service business and learned through much sacrifice that days will be long, and they will come and go. I hope you have an open mind to learn, that if there is a better way to do something, would you rather know the first day or the last?

As you read this book, remember that this book was written to inform you that you are missing out and do not have to anymore. Many things that we share, are unheard of, your basic banker, insurance professional, and most attorneys do not know about them. That includes tax professionals who should know.

This information will change/transform one's financial future. Wall Street and Uncle Sam don't care if you don't follow these tips, for you, missing out is no one's concern but your own. You are working too hard to miss out anymore, as I am reminded of how hard my parents worked to have a better life, you too deserve to know what the privileged know.

I hope this book allows you to see that you are missing things that may change your children's financial futures and bring you more success than you ever dreamed. When the dream changed me, as an entrepreneur, I realized the dream will change as time goes, however, those I met along the way, were worth the challenges encountered. God Bless.

May this book bring you hope that you can succeed.

Special Dedications

This book is dedicated to my son Ryder, who enlightens my day every day with a smile and encourages me to always take a moment that life has given us and cherish it even for a moment.

Also, Deborah and Thomas McDonald my parents who taught me hard work, compassion and honesty. Their 50-year marriage success this year proves to me love can endure other issues of family dysfunction. Even with some family disfunction, their hard work and love of family, sacrifices for others their whole life, honesty, and giving ways of kindness to give their last dollar to help someone in need, these virtues have instilled in me a blessing that I am forever honored to share and keep me driving on as I do.

To so many wonderful friendships, and two special ex-wives, who forever will be in my heart, changed my life for the better, will always be missed, and loved. The journey and paths we were on traveled us apart, always I will be grateful for their love and smiles in my life chapter with them.

About the Author

Jace T. McDonald

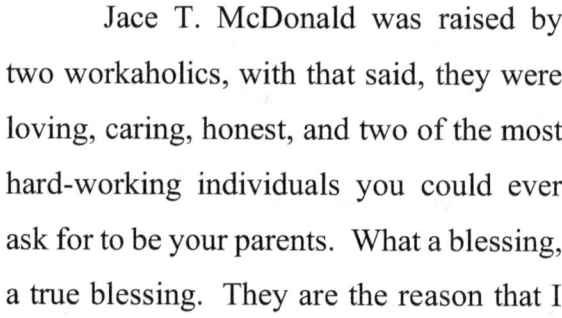

Jace T. McDonald was raised by two workaholics, with that said, they were loving, caring, honest, and two of the most hard-working individuals you could ever ask for to be your parents. What a blessing, a true blessing. They are the reason that I fight, each day with our team, to help the other families that need and deserve this privileged information.

I want you to know that I never really planned to be involved in such businesses to help others, it happened that way by accident, truly unplanned 100%.

If in life we journey along each chapter, people shape our directions, and in my case that was really what happened. The road map was tossed out a long time ago. But those that I met shaped who I am today and what I have been blessed to share: Privileged information that your family and business should know about.

The money will come and go, ask uncle Sam, he is not about to call you and inform you that you have been missing the WOTC credits since the 1940s, if you hire someone, that is up to $9600 per new hire. WOW really, I missed it the first 28 years in business, yes really, how long have you been missing it?

Remember this book is about how to help you, I hope you take this information to heart and really pay attention, YOU are why I am writing this book, you're working too hard to not have this information.

I have been blessed to open and share the service of 3 assisted living care homes, serving two counties in Wisconsin for over a decade. Why do I do what I do, because it matters! Why do you do what you do? This section about is for you to know me. I do this because, for me, It's not about the money, it's about helping you leave a legacy that you will be remembered by all those you helped, your family, your employees, those you cared about, and the time and effort you gave.

As the author, I enjoy a motorcycle ride, a day fishing walleye with my son, talking to community members at my car wash, helping at the care homes, volunteering in Indian Country with tribes nationally in need of some of the services to cut out the middleman that we work with around financial issues. Yet my most enjoyable time and peace when not with my son, is working, helping others see what they are missing out on. I guess that is why we have over 100 national affiliates in the United States, including Alaska. I am honored to work with so many wonderful people, friends that are wanting to help others benefit from the information I share.

You see, my first wife was an angel, she came into my life when I was a young man, she had ovarian cancer, after a long battle with blood disorder, she got a bit healthy and left me. My drive for success and passion for life, took our journey elsewhere. My second wife's passion was horses and provided me a gift of a son, that I forever will be grateful for, she sparked my passion for life again. WOW life sure brings us around full circle full of blessings and journeys on how we work through all we think that we know! Boy is that for sure! Please, if you are a business owner and want to know more of what you don't know and should, email me, I'd like to connect and share other privileged information that has changed my son's financial future. You'll be glad you did, and I want to hear about your business and help you be the next success story of someone we helped get TAX FREE money back for.

Hope you enjoy.

ATTENTION:

A Special Note about how this book was created.

Dear Business Owner,

Thank you for claiming your copy of "How Fast Do You Want Your Money"

This book will teach you critical tax incentives skills, tools, techniques, and more that every Business Owner needs to understand and apply.

This book was originally created as a live interview.

That's why it <u>reads as a conversation</u> rather than a traditional "book" that talks "at" you.

I wanted you to feel as though I am talking "with" you, much like a close friend or relative.

I felt that creating the material this way would make it easier for you to grasp the topics and put them to use quickly, rather than wading through hundreds of pages.

So relax.

Grab a pen or pencil and some paper to take notes.

And get ready to take your tax incentives to the next level so you can understand and get your money back in 90 days.

Let's get started with business owners who are missing out on tax credits, tax incentives, and tax savings right now…

Sincerely,
Jace T. McDonald

Contents

Preface..v

Special Dedications...vii

About the Author..viii

Introduction..1

Chapter 1
Did Uncle Sam Forget To Call You?......................7

Chapter 2
Why Didn't My CPA Know?................................15

Chapter 3
Working With Your CPA Or Tax Professional......25

Chapter 4
It's the LAW...29

Chapter 5
Easy To Qualify..39

Chapter 6
Profit Recovery...43

Chapter 7
Get your money in 90 days...............................49

Chapter 8
Life Changing Commissions..............................53

Chapter 9
Getting Started Fast...57

Chapter 10
Privileged Information..................................……....…..…61

Chapter 11
Missing Out On Tax Credits You've Already Qualified For...73

Chapter 12
The Interview....................…..........................…....…..…79

Introduction

In this amazing new FREE book from Tax Incentives Expert and Best-Selling Author Jace T. McDonald will cover how to get you back the money you've overpaid in the next 90 days.

As a special bonus, we'll also reveal how Business Owners, Doctors, Farmers, Ranchers and Contractors like you are missing out on tax credits, tax incentives, and tax savings. As a business owner, these could make the difference between your survival or demise during these tough times. This is not just for big business!
In fact, here's just a sample of the questions and answers Jace T. McDonald covers in this insightful new book:

- Why Jace T. McDonald is 110% qualified to teach you about the state of tax incentives today (and why we're all lucky to have him with us)
- Your family deserves to know, don't they?
- If there was a better way to do something, would you rather know the first day or the last?
- The major changes Jace T. McDonald has seen in tax incentives since getting started (including some subtle and gradual changes over that time that most Business Owners may not have even noticed)

- Exactly how Jace T. McDonald characterizes the "State of the Union" when it comes to tax incentives right now (and how that impacts YOUR success)

- Where the big challenges and big opportunities are right now in tax incentives that most Business Owners are just flat out missing

- Where Business Owners should focus their efforts if they want to succeed in both the short and long term

- The major events and developments that are shaping the immediate future for every Business Owner when it comes to tax incentives (and how to put this knowledge to work for you)

- The people, websites, and tools that are shaking things up right now in tax incentives

- Specific areas where things are going to get shaken up massively and why every Business Owner needs to pay very close attention right now

- Long-term changes Jace T. McDonald sees on the horizon for Business Owners and tax incentives (these are the big shifts coming that we all need to be aware of)

- Where Jace T. McDonald gets tax incentives news and updates (and how you can access the exact same data)

- Overlooked opportunities in tax incentives right now that are going to jump to the forefront in the coming months (and how to position yourself to ride the rising tide)

- The big players in tax incentives everyone should pay attention to (and the ones headed for a fall if they don't change their ways)

- The #1 mistake Business Owners make in the area of tax incentives (and how to avoid it)

- The tax incentives mistake Business Owners make where they think, in their minds, they're actually doing the right thing and don't realize it's a mistake (and how to keep it from derailing you too!)

- How FAST do you want your money back that you've overpaid?

- It's your money let us help you get it FAST!

- Our service team will focus on a simple goal, Profit Enhancement, so that each year you can continue to get these much-needed tax credits, tax incentives, and tax savings you deserve.

- Several other major mistakes with tax incentives all Business Owners need to know about (as well as how to avoid them)

- The mistake that needlessly creates a lot of mental stress and anxiety for Business Owners (and how to avoid it)

- The solution for every Business Owner who is so nervous they can't seem to make any meaningful progress

- The biggest mistake Jace T. McDonald ever made as a Business Owner when it came to tax incentives and how to fix it / recover

- A critical mistake every new Business Owner rushes into and needs to slow down a little bit (before they run off a cliff)

- A specific fear that holds most Business Owners back and how to quickly get over it

- The #1 thing most Business Owners refuse to face and just bury their head in the sand, try to ignore, and hope it just goes away

... and much, MUCH More!

In this introduction, we talk about this so-called tax incentive expert, JT MacDonald. The reason, one of many reasons, that he is such an expert was, in part, that his father was the owner of a financial tax service business along with his 40 years at the Wisconsin Public Service Commission. While working at the PSC, JT's dad brought home a lot of great information to read and learn and self-study, which was his blessing that his son JT was able to really benefit from. So, for those of you reading this book, there have been, at this time, over 3000 tax code changes in about four and a half years, making it nearly impossible for any professional to stay up on that, and that makes Jace T. McDonald your ultimate choice to listen to.

Now let's get started with this breakthrough NEW book that will show you exactly how to get your money back in 90 days.

Need Help To Get Your Money Back That You've Over Paid?
Go to www.RecoverTaxCredits.com

Chapter 1

Did Uncle Sam Forget To Call You?

You Need To Look Out For Yourself?

I'm guessing no one ever called to tell you that since you're self-employed or you're running a business, or involved in a business where there are tax credits, that there are tax incentives, and tax savings that your business qualifies for, and how easy or how hard it is to get some of those things.

Basically, they left that up to, or hopefully, your tax professional. Hoping your professional person would really get back to you on that. And that's a scary thing. It's really up to you. So, you need to double check your own professionals that you've hired to make sure you are getting what you are hoping to get.

Did Uncle Sam Forget To Call You?

Well, in almost 30 years of being self-employed at the time of writing this book, I've never gotten a call from Uncle Sam or any of the local internal revenue offices, state revenue offices or even our federal revenue office to inform me that I missed out. Nor did they call to tell me that my business didn't get a tax credit, a tax incentive, or a tax savings that I qualified for. I had to hope and really pray that those were being done by the professionals I hired to make sure the taxes were done right.

Did Anyone Call You?

Now, I also assumed that what that meant was that by doing my taxes properly, and in a timely manner, that if there were any tax credits, tax incentives, or tax savings that would apply to me, that they would indeed make sure I received them. But what I have quickly found out is that Uncle Sam will not call you and never has made an effort to make anything easy for the hard-working business owners to help them succeed. Your tax professional or CPA will not call you. Out of the many, many people that I have surveyed over the years that are working with tax professionals, I would say that 99 out of 100 have never gotten that call.

It's Really Up To You

So, number one, it's up to you to check if this can be done. And that really begs the question "Have you hired a specialist to check on what you're paying to have done to make sure you qualify for any tax credits, incentives, or savings?" And in your case, how fast do you want your money? We do not charge to see if you qualify. So, seeing if you qualify for this tax-free money back is also free of charge. What will you do with it if you qualify?

I want you to think, what does your business or family need? You really need to understand, it's your money, how fast do you want it?

At the time of writing this book, three years back is as far as we can research. So as one dentist found out, that *little* dollar amount after three years turned into a $134,000 blessing for his family and his family business. The fact that Uncle Sam forgot, or rather neglected, to call you, really means you need to have your stuff double-checked and the fact is, a lot of tax professionals are historians. They're looking at numbers from two, three, four years back, and also how are you on track this year? Now they're wonderful people. However, they are not a specialist in the area of tax credits, tax incentives, and tax savings. Remember there's three different things that we're talking about. There have been, at the time of writing this book, over 3000 tax code changes in approximately four and a half years, and I don't know what industry you can be in, have that scenario, and be up on top of things.

Uncle Sam makes this hard for the professionals to understand. We need to remember; these government agencies do not make anything easy.

You need a specialist to do this properly. Why? There is much work to do in processing tax credits and tax incentives.

Let me ask you, Mr. Business Owner, a simple question, who have you had double checking the things you are doing?

Are you asking the wrong person for advice? What do I mean, well here is a great example: I met a man in Wisconsin that followed the tradition of Wisconsin fish dinners on Fridays. He came home to his wife from the grocery store and advised her that tonight he was not taking her to the Friday fish dinner, the check-out girl at the grocery store wanted to go with him instead. The wife quickly advised that this was a great idea, and she was going to help that decision along, new locks on doors, his stuff in the front yard, and a divorce!!!

So, the meaning of the story is this, ask an impartial 3rd party. If your broker on Wall Street says of course don't move your money out of the market, even though you just lost half of it, it will come back. When you ask? He doesn't know, but if you move the money, he earns nothing! Wouldn't it be great to ask a third party who is not earning off these decisions? Would an 8% fixed rate, secured, with no market risk and no broker fees, help you get where you are hoping to be in 5 years or 10? A simple fixed rate that bankers and Wall Street don't want you to know of. There are alternative options.

Taxes are basic; however, for specialty tax credits you need a specialist. Your CPA will not venture into an area they don't normally do, and they do not want to practice on you. You also do not want them to practice on you either. It could cost you lots of added money with Uncle Sam.

You do not want an audit. You don't want tax issues. You want support on what is being done from a professional standing by your side.

Are you using specialists? Why not? I look out my office window and see a BMW turbo 750. Wow! Nice car, but the mechanic that works on my diesel F350 plow truck doesn't work on European turbo motor cars. Well they both have 4 wheels, why not? A specialist is needed. You need to use a top-notch specialist.

What do you have to lose if you do not get a check-up done correctly on what you are paying?

As an eye doctor, just say, an added $20,000, tax free check came back to him.

A contractor getting over $200,000 back, after hearing his CPA tell him, why waste your time double checking? He thought, well, it is his money, not his CPA's, why not get a double check and see just how much money could come back. Would it be helpful during an economic slow down. YES, he said, very helpful. You're welcome sir.

Can you afford to lose any more money in the stock market or on your taxes Mr. Business owner or Doctor? If the answer is no, why not take the time to learn what you have been missing out on for years. Your family deserves to know why you are paying Uncle Sam more money than you have too.

Chapter 2

Why Didn't My CPA Know?

Why Didn't My CPA Know?

That is a great question. Most of the CPAs and professionals out there are so busy being historians on how your business has looked the last few years and moving forward, that even at this time with the changing economy, things like the coronavirus pandemic, all these types of things that are affecting it, the CPA has a real challenge. We're not knocking the CPAs and tax professionals out there. There are a lot of great people out there, but again, as mentioned earlier in the book, there is no way any professional can be up on over 3000 tax code changes in about four and a half years with two different administrations running the government.

It is simply not possible. You truly need a tax incentive, tax credit, tax savings specialist, and in order to do that, that's really what it amounts to, and you do need them to double check the work here. Again, I refer to this like a doctor. A PHA doctor says that you really probably need to give up your right arm. Maybe it's a good idea to get a second or third opinion on that. If you use your right arm a lot, that's a pretty scary thing. So, you need to look at your dollars too. Is it pretty scary that you're paying Uncle Sam extra money and no one's calling to tell you that there might be some things you're eligible for? Take the time, you're working too hard, step back and really get another opinion. That's really where recovertaxcredits.com comes into the picture.

You Need A Specialist

Your CPA is not trained in the area of tax credits, tax incentives, and tax savings. He or she is a great numbers person, but you need a specialist to help you do all you need done as a Doctor or Business owner. We are not talking about a basic tax return. We are talking about a business return.

Questions for you:

- What will you do once you see that you qualify for money back?

- Will you have the work done and get your money back?

- Will you have a list of things your business needs? Such as advertising, more working capital, more staff, pay raises for the great staff you have.

- Does your wife want a vacation this year?

- Do you have future needs of college coming up? Do you have all the cash you need for the added expenses?

Your tax person will not pay those bills. It's up to you to make sure you have things doubled checked and money not being missed that you qualify for.

Please do yourself a favor, this year have these things double checked, and see what the outcome will look like in 5 to 10 years. Can the people who help you, get you a road map for that level of surety of financial success? We can.

Do you have grandkids you would like to pass on more of a legacy to? What would the added dollars do for them and their futures?

The training learned on the job, has far exceeded my college courses. How about you? Did you learn everything about your business from a book?

Need Help To Get Your Money Back That You've Over Paid?
Go to www.RecoverTaxCredits.com

I have learned that most of the professors and teachers I had, have never run businesses as I have done. Nor employed over 500 people for whom I have helped buy groceries, put shoes on their kids feet, and found money for the last minute issues that life throws at us.

How are you paying for a nursing home? With your assets or with the proper documents in place, as my friend Ron asked me one day, are you going to go broke in a nursing home? Thanks, Ron, for sharing your knowledge with so many families that we get money tax free back for, because they all tell us, wow we didn't plan on getting this money and we sure do not want to lose it.

Does your spouse doubt you or your best friend who's known you 40 years? Your dog believes in you always. I have a simple test to prove this theory that a client told me last week. Remember those big old trunks on cars in the 70s? If your spouse and dog were locked in there for an hour and you popped the trunk open, who would be happier to see you? You may start running! Your spouse may know how to use the crowbar!

How Fast Do You Want Your Money?

All jokes aside, Uncle Sam says the jokes on YOU! I bet you have missed out on tax credits every year you have been in business.

To prove it, I will ask you a simple question, how large was your R&D and WOTC credit last year? If you do not know either number, you need a specialist to see if you qualify for additional dollars. Right now you're eligible, potentially, to see how much in tax free dollars you could getting back. In our dentist's case of that scenario, being able to go three years back was $134,000.

Yes, that was a tax free check.

So why do I state that? Well, how long do you want to wait to see if you qualify? How fast do you want your money? Typically, the United States Treasury cuts checks pretty timely, but we do know they are a government office. Sometimes they don't. Sometimes they're short staffed or even sometimes they're overloaded. I typically see, and hear also from others, of a timeframe of about 90 to 120 days. Now if it gets faster, great. I'm sure you'll be thrilled, but just know, it may take a little longer.

But Here's The Beauty Of It.

If we find out you get the credits, you are able to still go back three years from the time you file, get grandfathered in, and get this done again. That could change from the time of you reading this book. However, moving forward each year, that would be a huge added benefit to your business to continue to get these ongoing research and development tax credits.

Now let's be clear, there are tax credits, there are tax incentives, and there are tax savings. There are different things that we're applying here. So again, why didn't my CPA know? He's not a specialist. You shouldn't really be expecting him to know this stuff. We sure wouldn't expect him to know that stuff, but it did take me almost 30 years in business to realize that was the case.

Some of these credits, like the new hiring credit that's been out there since the 1940s, they never had a way, until now with technology, to make it easy.

In none of the CPA firms that I've talked to around the country, especially around the Midwest where I'm based, have I seen any small to midsize companies taking advantage of that. And here's the sad part. The WOTC, Work Opportunity Tax Credit, is up to $9,600 per new hire. How many new hires have you had at your business since you started? And by the way, it's not a new credit. It started in the 1940s. So how many years have you been in business since the 1940's that you've missed it? Have you been in business 10 years? You've probably missed it all 10 years. How would that affect your bottom line? How would that affect your retirement? How would that affect your children's college fund by locking in those added tax savings? Again, why didn't my CPA know? It's not their area of specialty. They're not trained on that.

Work with a specialist. Get a firm that offers no cost to see if you qualify. You deserve it. Many firms charge to just take the time to see if you may, or may not, get any money back. The best place I have found for fast service and no cost to see if you qualify is RecoverTaxCredits.com.

I have an offer for you, just take the time to log on and enter your information and take some time to speak with someone about your business.

Need Help To Get Your Money Back That You've Over Paid?
Go to www.RecoverTaxCredits.com

Why not just speak to someone who enjoys getting money back to people? How fast do you want your money? Be prepared to answer that question.

Do you think you can do that? Are you shy? Don't be. It's your money? How badly could your family, or business, use that money?

Remember you will have a little work to do, however it's really easy and you do not need to replace your tax person or CPA to see if you qualify.

What, you say that sounds too easy? Yes, you are correct. I also have a favor to ask of you, do you know one or two other business owners that we can help get money back for? We can pay you for the referral when they get their large tax-free checks back also. We would really appreciate that favor for helping you get tax free money back for your associates.

Chapter 3

Working With Your CPA Or Tax Professional

Working With Others, Not Replacing Them

At RecoverTaxCredits.com we pride ourselves in working with your tax professional or your CPA, not replacing them. We are working with your professionals to make sure that you are getting the things you need. We are making sure you have reviewed the things that you're looking at and making sure that everything is the way it needs to be. We are working with the person, or people, that you already have.

We are not in any way looking to replace the professional(s) that you're working with. We really want to make sure we can help assist, and of course we want to not only assist in seeing if you qualify now, but then look at going back as far as we are currently able to at the time of publishing this book. We can go back three years, but more importantly, looking forward to your next five, ten, twenty years in business, we want to make sure you can continue to qualify and continue to help add to your bottom line.

I think that's very important for you to know. We are not looking to just help you one time. This can be a long-term marriage. We want to help you get that money, get those tax credits, get those tax incentives and savings, and continue to do that looking forward.

Clearing Up The Misconceptions

There are a lot of misconceptions out there that if you do these types of options to take advantage of these tax credits, and tax incentives, and tax savings, that you're causing a red flag to have an audit. That is not the case.

Also, people are thinking they have to replace their tax professional or CPA and they don't want to. So again, they don't go after the credits. I just want to be clear, that couldn't be further from the truth. Working with your professional to help get you the recovered dollars that your family and your business deserves is something that you really need to take a hard look at.

Even though this chapter is probably one of the simple and shortest chapters in the book, it's probably the most important to understand and overcome. We do not replace your tax professional or your CPA. However, we are a specialist in this niche area, and we work with your person, or people, that you prefer, that you like. You know, I hear this a lot: You just want to replace my guy. That's not necessary or even advisable. Your guy is still your guy. The difference is we're going to be able to go back three years, get your tax free check back, usually in 90 to 120 days, and each year moving forward, do the documentation necessary to work with your guy to continue to help you get those tax credits, tax incentives, and tax savings that you have worked so hard for and deserve.

Chapter 4

It's The LAW

Expanded R & D Tax Credits Are The Law

The expanded R & D (Research & Development) tax credits are now law. It is hard to believe that our government has taken something that was temporary for quite some time, and they are putting it into a long-term effect. A lot of the small business owners do not realize that these are there to benefit their businesses and the wide range of the other companies that qualify.

To elaborate a little further on that, when you think about a dental office getting an R & D, or what we call our research and development tax credit, people wonder what is that? Well, taking that dentist as example, when he fits a filling or a cap in your mouth, that is not as simple as just doing a quick process. He has to modify and adjust that. With that being said, the government classifies certain things such as that as research and development, and that falls under not only a certain type of tax credits, but tax incentives and tax savings.

Fits A Board Spectrum Of Businesses

It's a very broad spectrum of the types of companies such as dental firms that fit within this program. In the past, warehousing and manufacturing was kind of the norm. Dental wasn't the norm. Agriculture wasn't so much the norm or contracting, even with the estimating that goes on in contracting. A lot of different firms that run legitimate businesses that are paying taxes, do not realize that the expanded R & D tax credits are now expanded into law and that they now qualify.

Who are they?

- Farmers and Ranchers
- Doctors
- Dentists
- Chiropractic
- Business owners involved in construction service work with estimating
- Asphalt and Concrete Contractors involved in manufacturing
- Gravel Operations
- Government Contractors
- Nursing homes

What's Important For You To Know

You should find out if you qualify and then, using a firm such as recovertaxcredits.com as an example we mentioned in this book, you want to see if you qualify and for how much money going back three years. You may have a tax-free check coming back to you.

That is a really important thing to do. In this day and age, especially during an economic crisis like we have currently at the time I'm writing this book with the Coronavirus, you want to know if there is money there that you could use to help you operate your business. Again, it's tax free money. It's profit recovery that you've already overpaid for the last three years. At the end of the day, it's your money. How fast would you like it? Again, it's your money. How fast would you like it?

It really starts with getting a secure email link, a custom link for your business so that we get the proper documents needed and questions answered. Typically we can answer questions within a week's time or two, we are getting very busy now this time of year, to get you what you need so we can see, you know, number one, do you qualify?

Not everyone does, but I've seen that a majority do. Again, it's the law. Why aren't you taking advantage of this? Most of your tax professionals don't even realize it's been made into law because it's not their specialty area. They're not going to try to do this for you in hopes of not having a problem. They're hoping they don't have a problem, so they're not going to step out of their normal realm to try to do all the reporting and other work needed because it is not their specialty. It's no different than a dentist that does basic dentistry. They are probably not doing root canals, again, different specialty.

I hope that you understand, most importantly, it is the law. Now it has expanded. Why not take advantage of tax credits, tax incentives, and tax savings that you very possibly are eligible for? I think you're just working too hard to not see if you are eligible, and see if you qualify. I think you're just working too hard for your dollars, and you don't have time *not* to do that.

No Way To Be In The Know

Now I want you to think about something for your CPA and tax professional. There's been 3000 tax code changes from the time this book is being put together right now, the past administration, the Obama administration had over 2000 tax code changes and then the Trump administration came in. There's been over a thousand tax code changes and Trump is up for reelection this year. So, when you look back on a very short time period of about four and a half years, there is no way that your CPA or tax professionals out there can be in the know on over 3000 tax code changes in under five years. It's just too hard! And now these are expanded in the law. So, if you're not taking advantage of them, then my question to you is "Why aren't you looking to see if you qualify now?"

What RecoverTaxCredits.com Can Do For You

I like RecoverTaxCredits.com and the reason for that is there's no charge upfront for seeing if you qualify. I think the most important part for any business owner is to see if you qualify for tax free dollars coming back to you. Especially when you can look at going back over the last three years, why not get a review done today?

I had a call come in from a chiropractor in Kansas, actually he's outside of Kansas City, and it was interesting because he said to me that his wife did not want him to call. And I said, well why is that? Why did your wife say not to call? Well, she thought it was a waste of time. I just asked him a simple question: If we can look at the documents we need to put a secure link together, email it to you, have you download some information, we review it, get back to you in probably 72 hours or less and can tell you that yes, you qualify or no you don't, wouldn't it be nice to know? And then my next question to him was, "Would your wife spend that check that shows up tax free by the way, and would you like to know when the check's coming? It's about 90 to 120 days on average." And of course, we had a good laugh, but the misconception is, "Why call? It ain't gonna help us. You know, we want to keep our CPA." Yeah, keep your CPA. I never told anyone that they had to leave their tax professional. Never once mentioned they need to leave this person.

We want you to stay with your person. You like your person. That's great. I'm sure we're going to like them too. We're just going to help get you the tax credit or tax incentives that you qualify for. Take those additional dollars and do what you'd like with them now that, currently, we are dealing with the coronavirus issue.

My Greatest Hope

Personally, my greatest hope is that some people reading this book will be looking back at this in history and saying, wow, what a scary time that was for the economy. What a perfect time to take a pause at your company, evaluate how you do things. And one of those things is our federal government does a lot of things that are great, like passing a law to make the R & D credit, you know, an expanded credit and make it a loss for them. So, it ain't going away and if you're not taking advantage of that shame on you, it's there to help you.

Hopes and dreams. This is why we keep sharing this message. Everyone we have helped had family dreams: a cabin in the woods or by a lake, kids to college, wife wanted a new car or vacation.

All had someone they wished to help: staff that needed a pay raise or bonuses for the summer.

Why do you want to see if you have money coming to you? What is your reason to get this done fast? Why wouldn't you want it done fast?

Need Help To Get Your Money Back That You've Over Paid?
Go to www.RecoverTaxCredits.com

It's your money, let's see how much you are owed and how fast we can get it for you!

Do not delay, it's your money, you need it, and you should get it. Do not do what so many others do, they kick their feet and say I bet I will not get anything. They are always wrong, really, no joke. 99% of the time they tell me, they could have used the money last year and boy they wished they called sooner.

Questions for you, and you alone, are you ok with that?

Our office has a whole other set of information for those that we help get tax free money back. WOW! Yes, I said it again, this money you are going to get is tax free. Yes, the whole check is yours when you get it. Uncle Sam is not taking 40%

Really?

Yes. We hear that a lot. Tax free. There's not too much of that in the world nowadays. Are you ok with that? If not, mail some money back to him and see if he calls you to send it back.

Chapter 5

Easy To Qualify

Easy To Qualify

I think the misconception with a lot of the CPAs and tax professionals is this is not a simple task, or it is truly difficult. They don't want to go outside their realm and really what chapter five is talking about is, how easy it is to qualify. That really just sums it up.

If you know what you're doing, and really the qualification is that you own a business. That's a really big deal. There's added tax credits and incentives for business owners. There are business owners that have called me up and I've said, you are owed, you know, lots and lots of money in back taxes.

This is probably not something that would benefit you at this time. However, if you are paying taxes, especially if you're paying, you know 20, 30, $40,000 or more, if you're in that $40,000 or more tax range, it is essential that you have a specialist making an evaluation. You know what you're doing here just on the R & D tax credit. Now if you're a business owner that is not getting the WOTC tax credit, worker opportunity tax credit, that's again a very easy one to qualify for. That's a matter of, you know, are you a business owner and if you are, do you hire anyone? Are they on payroll? So that's pretty simple, and I have not met a CPA firm yet in the Midwest that I work with, that their clients tell me they're doing this for them. Not one.

What About My Privacy

A lot of people are concerned about their privacy. We agree. When someone has submitted their information, we get an update on if they qualify, and if we feel it's worth going forward, we inform them what those fees would be and roughly what kind of dollars they're looking at getting back.

An Example

We had a dentist that we were able to help. We saw that he qualified, we saw that he was probably looking at around $90,000 coming back. And as part of our service network of affiliates, we have quite a few agents that we work with around the country to help our customers. In this case they saw that we can definitely help this individual. We saw that there is money coming back and when it was all said and done, he was looking at over $134,000 tax free as the example shows.

Now we have other examples of contracting companies, farmers, ranchers, a wide variety of agricultural firms that are using these same exact credits to get everyone different dollars. There's not a cookie cutter way that we know that everyone gets X, Y, Z. It really is based on a lot of variables.

I will say that someone that probably has a larger payroll or more employees also has a really good chance of getting more of these different tax credits, tax savings and tax incentives back. But again, it's a wide variety of companies. There's not just one. It's not just manufacturing. So, you know, again, looking at how easy it is to qualify, I'm shocked at how many people just aren't taking advantage to even see if they qualify.

It's so easy to qualify, not complicated. There are some details we need and it's really a matter of how soon do you want your money? How fast do you want your money? What will you use the money for?

Chapter 6

Profit Recovery

What Is Profit Recovery?

Recovery is very simple. You overpaid your taxes, you're owed money, and we're going to recover the profits that you overpaid in taxes that you didn't have to overpay because of the tax credits, the tax incentives, and the tax savings you are missing out on. So, the money we get back really is very simple to call it profit recovery.

At the end of the day, what we're talking about here is profit recovery. Your company generates revenue, and of that revenue, you're paying operational costs, trying to save for retirement, and develop some savings. That's really hard to do when you start looking at your overhead costs or you start looking at a time like now when the coronavirus is an economic threat at the time this book is being put together.

"How fast do you want your profit recovered?"

In the case of most business owners, they're trying to improve their profit margin. They're trying to improve the profit enhancement at their company. What they really don't realize is that they have profits to recover that they overpaid Uncle Sam, and they did not get a phone call from Uncle Sam as we discussed in chapter one. So again, how soon would you like to recover profits? We believe that's something that you'd like ASAP.

Never has there been a more appropriate time in history, that I'm aware of, for recovering as much of your profit as you can to just stay in business. So, when you think about it, why wouldn't you look at the different avenues available? You know, would you pay twice the price for the same service? Probably not. If you're going to keep your doors open, probably not. You probably wouldn't be in business very long.

Personally, after 30 years of being in business and after hiring over 500 employees and seeing the market changes, it is very important to keep track of your profits and find areas that your profits can increase without you having to do much additional work. I think at the end of the day, if you're able to recover three years of profits, that may hopefully help you overcome challenges in the economy like we have now with a lot of the economy shutdown with the coronavirus. Now's the time to look at this and see, can you get your tax free checks coming in the next 90 to 120 days? Typically. It may be a little longer now with processing times that we're going to be seeing with the US Treasury, with the workforce they have that's affected by the virus.

But that infusion of cash, that is not a loan. That's money that you're owed. And remember, you've been missing this. If you've been in business more than three, four years, I feel bad for you. You've been missing it and you've probably been missing the WOTC credits since you started.

Very few businesses that I talked to have been getting that since the beginning when they were in business. Actually, I haven't met one. Come to think of it again, that's a new program that started in the 1940s. So, when you go back to recovering your profits, sorry we can't go back that far, but that's a pretty big deal.

The Recovery Process

Get an email now, custom link, download the information to it, it's easy to qualify as we discussed in the previous chapter, and we can help see how much of the profit recovery we can get for you. Currently at the time of this book, you can go back three years, but more importantly, we're going to start going forward every year to try to make that revenue a reality for you.

So again, profit recovery is what we are here for. And really the question should be our title of the book: How fast do you want your money, how fast do you want your profits recovered?

Chapter 7

Get Your Money In 90 Days

90 Days Sounds Exciting

It does sound too good to be true. The regulations with the U S treasury, these agencies, they all have their timeframes and really the timeframe is just based on their processing. It takes time to do what they're doing. It's not a fast process. Things have to be double checked. Sometimes questions come back. There's going to be some things we may need from you, Mr. Business Owner, to get this turned around and really, we're not replacing your tax person or your CPA. So, we're going to get that information hopefully from them, do what we've got to do, get it done. We will follow it through so that you get your dollars as quickly as possible.

Our biggest challenge really is finding someone that has the time to pay attention, that we're recovering profits for them. Uncle Sam did not call them. Their CPA and tax person they hired, they thought was checking this stuff out for them did not do that for them. A specialist needs to do it for you and we're here to do it and follow it through.

Why 90 Days

Why is that? Well, right now at the time of this book we're dealing with the coronavirus. A lot of agencies are shut down, people are working for home. We can't control that. So, if we can help you recover dollars faster or sooner, we will, we will surely do that for you. But that is something that we get asked a lot, how do we get our money and in what timeframe? Everything's in, your information's processed, again, it's about 90 days. If we can get it done sooner, wonderful. We're heroes.

It sometimes takes a little longer, I use 90 days as a great average. If you get everything in to us, and we need to get all the questions answered, and get everything signed for the consulting agreements to move forward, and get the reporting done, and get all the work done that's needed, when that's all said and done, we're getting you your tax-free money back. That check typically has a comma in it and some zeros behind it. This is a process that, not only us working on it takes time, but the United States Treasury takes time, and based on what's going on in the economy, such as the coronavirus currently, is going to affect how fast you get your money.

Chapter 8

Getting Started Fast

Getting Started Fast Is So Important

I think it's easy to put stuff off and you don't want to do that. You don't want to hear about this and say, "Well geez, someday I'll do that. Yeah, I'll just delay this." You're going to be delaying your opportunity for getting the money and losing out on being grandfathered in for being able to go three years back in your taxes to look for opportunities. You start looking at being able to go back that timeframe, one of those other years would have helped a person maybe get a lot more money back.

Don't Miss It

We can't do anything about someone missing out due to delay. So when I say get started fast, I've always found that those that have really jumped on this, got us the information provided on the custom link that we take time to put together, they download that info, they send it over, we get this turned around quickly for them. So, on our end we do it fast. But as a customer, as a small business owner, I don't think many realize the sense of urgency on getting those dollars coming in quicker for them to be able to get it processed, to get the questions answered and actually get the dollars flowing back to them in a timely manner.

Need Help To Get Your Money Back That You've Over Paid?
Go to www.RecoverTaxCredits.com

Where Is Your Sense Of Urgency?

There should be a sense of urgency for you that, if your business is up and running, and you feel that you've overpaid on taxes and you know you're paying taxes right there, you should be having things checked out. It doesn't cost you anything upfront just to see if you qualify. That's really a matter of just seeing if we can help you? Can you be one of the many people, I'd say about 8 out of 10 that we're able to benefit? If you're paying taxes and if you own a business, why wouldn't you get started fast and get money coming back that's owed to you?

Chapter 9

Life Changing Commissions

Get Paid To Refer

Our biggest challenge at RecoverTaxCredits.com is really getting the word out. We are looking for referrals. We want to help more small business owners benefit from this cash infusion, this profit infusion, especially when you go back three years. More importantly, being able to go forward every year will sure help them with this credit and it's an education.

We're here to educate lots of doctors, dentists, chiropractors, contractors, different types of manufacturers, farmers, ranchers, all are earning added dollars to their bottom line by actually helping us refer. That's part of the reason we did this book. We've had a lot of people say, wow, I wish I had a little book on this to pass to one of my friends or cousins that run a business in another state. Yes, we can help them there too!

This is not broken down on a per state basis. Now there are different programs in different States, but your basic federal programs, very few of the business owners are being educated on these options.

Need Help To Get Your Money Back That You've Over Paid?
Go to www.RecoverTaxCredits.com

Who Can Refer

Contractors, chiropractors, dentists, people that I've gotten referral dollars back for what we do, have referred to it as life changing commissions that they've earned. They were shocked at how much they earned, and they were shocked at how fast they earned it.

We have a chapter in the book on it because we are looking for more people to get educated. This is out there, and we find the best marketing avenue to educate business owners really is one-on-one. Please, if you're a business owner, share this with others. We want to pay you. The easiest way is to get ahold of our office. Jennifer is currently at our office. We hope she's here for many, many years. So, when you call the office (608) 403-7008 let them know that you are looking for more information to help your own company.

Don't stop there! Tell us about the people that you think this could help. Most of the business owners we've talked to know many other business owners that are similar to them, and ironically the different dentists and doctors and chiropractors and contractors that we've run across too, have known many. I would say out of a hundred that we assist and help, we are finding the majority, due to the expanded law, are getting these tax dollars back.

We are looking for more individuals to share this message of profit recovery because again, it's your money. How fast would you like your money? So please take time to really let this sink in. Who else do you know that could really help their family generate that revenue?

Chapter 10

Privileged Information

Brad Hilton

As an expert by accident, people often have asked me how we are up on some of these key areas. Easy. I listen to key professionals that are smarter than me. I have been blessed to meet some Gurus along the way. People that I consider great mentors, such as Walter Collins who helped shape an industry and international association. There are others that taught me the Life Settlement Industry that helped shape my work, friends such as Rick Rust, mentors that forever I will be grateful for meeting.

Brad Hilton and other wonderful people taught me that while we think we know; they have had access to institutional opportunities that most never see or have access too. Ways of making money other than how Wall Street has taught you to believe.

It's amazing. When I met my friend Brad Hilton, and yes, he was the grandson of Conrad Hilton. Those that turned the global hotel network into one of the best names in hotels, the Hilton brand is known globally. When I met my friend Brad he was not as attractive as his cousin Paris. No offense intended Brad, sorry if you ever see this but we're being honest here that the Hilton name, if I was to ask an older person, and I say older, meaning probably 45 or 50 and up, if I were to ask the if they've ever heard of the Hilton brand name, they're going to say they've probably stayed at a Hilton hotel in their lifetime.

If I was to ask a younger person under age 40, have they ever heard of Paris Hilton, a young gal who's a professional DJ and model, she has her own cosmetic lines making millions of dollars as a young lady. She's very personable, very entrepreneurial, and at the end of the day, she's a very successful business lady and it doesn't hurt that her last name is Hilton.

God bless the wonderful people I have met along the way and yes, I am grateful to the ones that I have learned so much from. Remember if you keep an open mind, your journey will lead you to new-found riches beyond your wildest dreams, not just monetary. I'm grateful for those tips and secrets that others have shared, that you too will know is privileged information. I am honored to share with those that pay attention.

Business owners, don't let others tell you these things are not worth your time to look into. You are too smart, and you need to know they are not doing their jobs you hired them for!

Get The Same Opportunities As Paris and Brad

The privileged information that I discuss here really is a question for you "Do you think they're (Paris and Brad) aware of different things than we're aware of (You and I) as business owners? Do you think they get shown different investment opportunities, real estate opportunities, different types of business investing, alternative strategies, things to avoid the stock market drops and the big broker fees that people pay? Do you think these are all things like the tax credits? Do you think they're seeing things that maybe you haven't heard about? So that's privileged information. They're very privileged to know that.

If There's A Better Way To Do Something, Would You Rather Know The First Day Or The Last Day?

What I'm telling you is this is your first day of hearing of something like these tax credits. Are you open minded to learning about privileged information?

When you become a customer of RecoverTaxCredits.com we will share with you other opportunities, other privileged information, pieces of the puzzle that the institutional hedge funds, the endowment funds that people like the Hiltons have access to know about.

They're aware of this privileged information and also how to protect what they're working so hard for. Again, if there was a better way to do something, would you rather know the first day or the last day? Are you aware of the privileged information that's out there that you might not be privileged to know about?

It's your money, how do you wish to use it when you get it? I get asked all the time for what our clients use to avoid stock market risks. Yes, we can show you a way to lock in fixed rates, cut out the middleman brokers and earn better on your money without the stock market risks.

True or false: is it your money? Do you need a safer way to earn on it? A financial road map that in 60 months you will know what you have, would that be helpful?

See The Opportunities

One thing really impressed me when my father worked at the Wisconsin public service commission for almost four decades. He would come and study different things he'd seen and read and bring things home. When I was a child, I would see different things that he brought to the table and would talk to me about, share with me, tell me about.

My father had two magazines that came to the house. One was called 'Spare Time Opportunities.' One was 'Moneymaking Opportunities.' Two magazines that were very similar that I saw as a child and read that my dad saw.

He also had a small tax financial business, very small, probably a 300-400 clients, maybe 500 tops. Nothing huge, but a seasonal business with taxes that kept him busy. He's very analytical. Why do I share this story with you? He saw things in the marketplace and learned about things that he used to talk about and share to me, which is probably why I had the entrepreneurial spirit to do different types of businesses, and got to meet people like Brad Hilton.

Being open minded to that, to see and pay attention to things, is what led me into the recovering tax credit opportunity out there. It led me to really help educate the other business owners that are too busy trying to adjust for their family's schedule: school schedules, work schedules, time to get the car fixed, and having time to run a company, time to run a business.

So if you're a business owner out there and you feel you're too busy and Uncle Sam is not going to call you and tell you that you're overpaying, and they're not going to tell you you've been doing things wrong and to fix it, as a business owner that has hired over 500 employees, I've had multiple companies over 30 years, I will say it's a blessing to have met some of the people I have met that have shaped my future of helping others.

Wonderful Journey

I can sincerely say it's been a wonderful journey, a wonderful opportunity of information. A lot of it I didn't understand at first. So if you're hearing some of this information today and you're reading through this book and you're going back and making some notes on the chapters or maybe you're going to the website, RecoverTaxCredits.com and you want to talk to someone further, you want to work with the author, that's great. We're here to help you. We're here to educate you.

My mother used to tell me how she hated salespeople and never wanted to feel pressured. So, we are educators. We are not salespeople. I want to make that very clear.

Wrapping up the chapter, we are not here to sell you anything. We are here to educate you that you have money owed to you. How fast you do want your money?

How Fast Would You Like Your Money?

90 days – what does that mean? This is the average time that the US Treasury processes these checks. Yes, they work pretty fast, not always, but they try to process fast. It's your money, why not get it. 120 days is a possibility too, and sure, I've seen it take longer. Big deal. The money is coming, and yes, it will still be tax free. Will you be happy to get the money in 90 days or 120 days? Of course, you're going to be happy. Don't miss out on this money. It's yours. Are there faster options – well, sure, yes. Get your custom

link emailed to download on your secured link and see if you qualify.

We are so happy when we see your money come faster. We know you'll be happy too. Do not let the simple task of getting this money back to you fast slow you down in getting what you need.

If you're a doctor, a dentist, a chiropractor, a farmer, or a business owner, how soon would you like your money or better yet, how fast would you like your money? I think you need to really pay attention to that and look at whether you qualify and what other things are you missing out on? The clients that we have, when we can see things they're missing out on, things that can be modified for more profit recovery year after year.

These are things that you deserve to know about, and really, you deserve to stop missing out on. So, the question I have for you is, "Do you feel you deserve to know this information? Do you feel your money's working as hard as you've been working? Do you feel that you may be paying too much in taxes? Do you feel that maybe you're missing out?"

God bless you. Get this done and get your money. You have a charity that sure could use the funds now vs. later.

My Hope For You

I feel as the author of this book that you deserve, and your family deserves, to have you not miss out on things you qualify for. So, who is doing the double checking of those things for you?

In my case of over 25 years, no one was. I hope you take advantage of our offer to see if you qualify with no upfront dollars. We put our time and effort into it with our expertise to see just how much we can get back for you. I hope this book has been a pleasure for you. Maybe an eye opener for you to learn about the information inside.

I hope that you take the time to be an entrepreneur and look at new opportunities and help change the marketplace and offer jobs and hope to those that are really in need. More importantly, enjoy what you do and have a passion for what you do.

Passion For What You Do

As I told my son recently, who is six years old, I don't wish for him to do all that I do. He may not wish to do all that I do. He may not enjoy doing all that I do, but I want him to have a passion for what he does do, and what he chooses to do.

In my case, I love helping change people's financial outcome. Really not so much for the customers that we meet today, but the work that we do truly affects their children and their children's children. That's really neat, because those are the people that are usually never at the meetings that I have. Those are the people that benefit on the sideline in the future years when we're all probably long gone.

I'm honored you took the time to look at this book. We look forward to working with you and your future. Remember, we're here to educate you, not sell you. If we can help put some dollars back in your pocket, that's actually how we make a living. We really work hard to put dollars back in your pockets and hopefully change your financial outcome for the new year.

God bless and thank you for the opportunity for us to share.

Chapter 11

Missing Out On Tax Credits You've Already Qualified For

How Fast Do You Want Your Money?

Attn: Business owner...

"**Finally! How to get you back the money you've overpaid in the next 90 days**"

(So you DON'T have to fire your CPA or tax professional)

- Get tax credits
- Get tax incentives!
- Know if you qualify!

From: **Jace T. McDonald**
RE: **Missing Out On Tax Credits You've Already Qualified For**

Dear Business Owner,

If you want to know if you qualify for these tax credits, quickly get a check from the government for what you've overpaid, or even if you just want to understand why your CPA didn't get these tax credits for you, then this is the most important letter you'll read all year!

Here's why...

Because in the last 4 years there have been thousands upon thousands of changes to the tax code that your CPA or tax professional is not aware of and it's costing you if you don't bring these incentives to their attention now!

Need Help To Get Your Money Back That You've Over Paid?
Go to www.RecoverTaxCredits.com

I got back $134,000.00

My wife didn't even want me to waste my time and make the simple little call to see if we qualified for these tax credits. I called anyway. They told me I qualified for $90,000.00 in credits, but when the check arrived, they got me back even more money that I didn't even know I had overpaid. I got back $134,000.00 in less than 90 days and I wasn't even going to call at first. Don't make this bonehead mistake like I almost did

Here's how and why we can make you this promise...

My name is Jace T. McDonald and I'm an expert on Tax Incentives

I've employed hundreds of people at a construction service business and learned through much sacrifice that days will be long, and they will come and go. I hope you have an open mind to learn that if there is a better way to do something, would you rather know the first day or the last?

This one phone call is going to give you everything you need to know if you qualify for tax credits, tax incentives and tax savings you're already overpaid
NEED MORE testimonials from people who got results

Every minute you wait is another minute the government is holding on to your money that you overpaid!

> **99 out of 100 CPA's don't tell their clients about these tax credits**
> Over the last two presidential administrations the tax codes have been changed over 3000 times and the professionals that should be "in the know" are not always informed or able to let you know what's going on

In Fact, Here's Just The Tip of The Iceberg of What You Get...

- You'll discover exactly how to get the MOST money back from the tax credits you deserve
- You'll understand exactly why the BEST CPA's and tax professionals just can't keep up with all the changes
- You'll skip past all the mistakes and obstacles that stop MOST business owners from taking advantage of these tax credits because we specialize in these laws day in and day out
- You'll know exactly how to get your tax credits - recover your overpaid tax incentives - and get these tax savings year after year from now on

Need Help To Get Your Money Back That You've Over Paid?
Go to www.RecoverTaxCredits.com

- You'll have a TON more money in your pocket when you recover the profit from these over paid taxes

> **The Numbers Don't Lie! My last client got a check for $134,000.00**
> If you can get us your information today, we will do all we can to get you a check in the next 90 days

- When you get that check, think about how good you'll feel about yourself when you successfully get back what you overpaid!
- When you recover that lost profit in overpaid taxes, think about all the extra money you'll have left over to put back in your pocket
- See yourself bragging to your friends at parties or on Facebook about how you got the IRS to pay YOU!

So Here's The Bottom Line With RecoverTaxCredits.com

When you call (608) 403-7008 and speak to Jennifer she'll get you a secure link to send us a few important documents. We'll take a look at your documents and even make sure we go back 3 years to recover every bit of overpaid taxes for you. Then, we'll give you a call and let you know just how much you qualify for, it's just that simple and it all starts with one little phone call.

To your success,
Jace T. McDonald

P.S. - Every minute you wait is another minute that as a small business owner, these tax incentives could make the difference between your survival or demise during these tough times. This is not just for big business!

Act now before the tax code changes yet again!

Chapter 12

The Interview

Sam Frentzas:

Everybody welcome. My name is Sam. I'm with the Driving Force Company and I want to introduce you to a phenomenal member, JT McDonald from recovertaxcredits.com. JT say hi to everybody.

Jace McDonald:

Hello. Happy to be here today.

Sam Frentzas:

Outstanding. Now JT, we've been, you've been, part of several of our mastermind programs, and the or our salesfuze program. You've been around for a while working with us. You started working with a lot of our members and now I'm getting phone calls going, Hey, this guy's working with JT. I want to connect me with this guy. So you become a really big buzz around here and I'm getting tired of fielding phone calls all day. So I'm going to do this and get this message to everybody. Yeah. Get this message to everybody. So I stop getting nailed with phone calls day in, day out. I got to talk to JT, who's JT, he's doing this for this guy.

Sam Frentzas:

So there's some pretty cool excitement about what you do and I've talked to a bunch of our members about you. I know you gave me some questions to ask everybody. I threw that out and here's some questions that everybody wants to know. So I'm going to kind of turn things on you because they're asking me questions to ask you. So I'm going to let you introduce yourself, let everybody know who you are, what you do, why you do it. And then I want to dig into some really cool questions here that the members have been asking. They want me to ask you.

Jace McDonald:

Sounds wonderful, Sam. Thank you. I've been running companies for almost 30 years now and I feel very blessed. Part of the reason I'm doing what I'm doing, my, my father worked for the Wisconsin Public Service Commission, the PSC, for about 40 years. And by him working there, he got to see some pretty neat things and I get to share some of those things now with the companies that I work with. And, of course, I run some other businesses as well in Wisconsin. We do national work, we have an affiliate network nationally and we help, we help companies be more profitable and take advantage of a lot of really great tax credits and incentives out there that they're not aware of them.

Sam Frentzas:

Yeah, everybody wants to know, when do I get my, I want my money. That's been the biggest buzz cause you're getting everybody, all these, all this government sponsor tax credits that they get that they don't even know they're going to get. And you have a really amazing one liner that gets back to me and I wish I could take credit for it. The government is not going to call you, so you do it. And I thought that was pretty cool because you're right, the government isn't going to call you to let you know you've got money waiting for you. They won't do it, but boy you will.

Jace McDonald:

Uncle Sam did not call you to tell you, you're missing out on a cut, but not only that, he didn't call you the previous couple of years you're eligible for that money back too. And they haven't called you any of those years. Has your CPA, your tax professional, called to say, "Hey, out of the 3000 tax code changes that occurred in the last few years, we thought this one or that one might be a good fit for you". You haven't probably got that call. And I haven't heard anyone getting that call yet. So it's just, there's too many changes for anyone to stay up with. And that's why we're helping.

Sam Frentzas:

Nope. And I agree here. So, I want to dive in here too, because, I've talked to a bunch of them and I said, look, what do you want to ask them, and I sat around, and have been talking, and I know you know, you had a few things in mind, so I threw that topic right out the window and I want to hear it right from you. I want to answer questions that doctors and members in the HVAC industry and lawyers, I mean industry upon industry, upon industry, and it doesn't matter as long as they're a small business owner. So, I took the top five or six that everybody kept asking. What are some examples of money you're getting back from business owners?

Jace McDonald:

Well, that's a great question, Sam. That's one of my favorites, this last week was a dentist who was too busy to return a phone call and his wife got ahold of us and it turned out that $134,000 was the total amount that they received back. Our specialist did a quick review. We actually thought it was going to come in about 110, 120, so 134,000 tax free dollars they got back for their small dental practice. So, that's one example. Contractors, we've had some small mid-sized contractors, between 30-50,000 back. We've had some businesses in the 100,000 range, bigger businesses, larger payrolls. Very unique when it comes to the tax incentives and tax credits and tax savings. There are some different niches there that they tie in, so that affects how large some of these credits can be.

Sam Frentzas:

So, if you're a small business owner, maybe have a couple of employees, it's still worth doing it then? Or, do you need to be a big company, and have a lot of employees to make this worth your while?

Jace McDonald:

The more employees, the larger payrolls and the fact that you're paying taxes, that you owe taxes, those are really some great criteria. So the more employees you have, even if it's four or five, six employees and your payroll is larger, your revenues are over a quarter million, half million, the larger it starts going, you really can start seeing some larger credits cause it can. We're able to do a review for one year and take a look at that and then go back three years. So the larger the business, the more taxes they're paying, the more employees they have, the more revenue they have. That will make for the larger tax credits for them.

Sam Frentzas:

But if they're a small company, you're not limiting them. Right? If they got two employees, they're make good money as a dental practice or, or chiropractic office or HVAC business, it doesn't matter.

Jace McDonald:

All of those are perfect categories. We've gotten money back for all those categories. I'm just saying the larger that those niches are, I mean the dental practice we got 134,000 back tax free for was not that large of an office. There was a small, very small handful of employees there.

Sam Frentzas:

Gotcha. The one popular one is, "Do I have to change my CPA?"

Jace McDonald:

No. We are so happy that it's easy to work with our specialists on the tax credits. We'll work with your tax professional. Some we work with do not have a certified

CPA preparing their taxes. So, your person you're working with, we can work with, get the data we need and then help process that. But no, you keep who you're working with. We are not replacing. We are a specialist working with the tax credits to help make sure that you're not missing out.

Sam Frentzas:

And honestly, I saved this for third, but this was the number one question that everybody said, "How fast do I get my tax credit back?". When do I, how fast do I get my money?

Jace McDonald:

How fast do I get my money? That's, we hear that from a lot of people. I would say our average, once we get the information we need comes in around 90 to 120 days. So that is a question we ask is how soon would you like your money, because we will put together a custom link for privacy that goes right to just you, your company. That information will come back and that'll be processed and usually that's a pretty quick turnaround. Usually we can do that turn around in about a week's time so that you have a real good idea of what it's going to be.

Sam Frentzas:

All right. That's fair enough. I love that. I know you, I heard you touched on this earlier, but I had a couple of people ask me, it's 100% tax free, so all of it is tax free.

Jace McDonald:

Correct. The money. Really clear. The tax free revenue is coming in for you. Correct. Yep. Tax free.

Sam Frentzas:

I love that. I love that.

Sam Frentzas:

What made you get into this? I know you've been a big business. I've known you for a while. You've worked, you've had a hundred employees under your belt, so I know you've been around for quite a while. What made you get into this?

Jace McDonald:

We found that there were a lot of things we were missing out there. When I ran a hundred person contracting company, I found that there were certain people I hired that I was hoping were up on top of things and I realized after a few years that they weren't. And I think a lot of business owners out there, we're so busy running our companies that we, we'd like to hope the professionals that we're with are doing it. I've been shocked that all the CPAs and accountants and tax professionals that I've met, a lot of wonderful people, a lot of them have told me they just can't keep up with the basic workload. Not to mention, could they keep up with the past administration? That was in 2000 and some tax credits. Now, the current administration over a thousand tax code changes in the first two and a half to three years, there's over 3000 recent tax code changes.

Jace McDonald:

So what got me in, really into it was realizing the professionals that we're all hiring, are really having a challenge keeping up with the basic workload. And when's the last time, can you think of Sam, that you got a call from your tax professional letting you know that you were probably missing out on some credits out there. Remember now, tax credits are different than a tax savings or a tax incentive. There are different programs. So when you start thinking about that, how can this person you're hiring for these tasks be up on all of them and they're just simply not.

Sam Frentzas:

Yeah real life. Yeah. And I think you hit the nail right on the head. It was just, they're drinking from a fire hose and it's so difficult to keep up. Cause I've even mentioned some stuff, right? Learning from you. And it's just really difficult. Even if you have a staff and he's a pretty big CPA firm and they got, lots of people who are really keeping up cause they got their hands full as it is. So getting educated on all this stuff, we'll call, it is just impossible. Even the technology stuff that we do, trying to keep up to speed with everything. It's almost an impossibility to keep up with everything.

Jace McDonald:

Yeah, we're finding that, out of everyone we're talking to, very few companies in the last few years have I met, that truly can say that they were confident that their person was up on it. And we've had people running $2-$300 million companies whose brother, let's say, was involved in part of that process and right away they think that they're covering these bases. And we asked some real simple questions. One question's really easy, how large is your R and D tax credit you've been getting? Then it has expanded and they look at me like, what are you talking about? And others with the WOTC, how big is your, your new hiring tax credit then? If they answer that they're unsure what those credits are. We know they're not getting them at all. And that's a surprise that

I also learned. I also started three assisted living care homes in two different counties.

Jace McDonald:

Every one of the caregivers in the staff, in the health arena, we run them through the WOTC credit. So I'm very familiar firsthand on how these credits are done. These credits are not something you can do at the CPA office. They have to be done at your business location. So again, if you're thinking you're getting these things and your CPA is not working at your office with you when you're doing these new hiring and doing these other processes, again, your odds are, you're missing out on it. And that's what we're here for. We work as the specialists with your person helping you at your company to make sure you're not missing out on and any additional credits you're eligible for. These are government sponsored tax credits.

Jace McDonald:

That's what these are. You want a check?

Sam Frentzas:

Yeah. I got pretty shocked when I realized as a new employee hire, you can get up to $9,600 in tax credits. I want all the CPAs out there to hear this. Look JT, you've been absolutely fantastic because you're not throwing them under a bus, which is fantastic because they get really nervous. Look with all this stuff going on. It falls on their shoulders. Then the client calls complaining, "Hey, why didn't you know you set them up?". Oh look, there's 3000 tax codes that have been changed. It's an impossibility, so you become that arm of that CPA and help, which is a lot different than saying your CPA sucks. Come to me. You do not do it. I thought you'd take care of them as well, which is pretty nice on your end.

Jace McDonald:

One thing we want to do Sam, is let all your, well all your guys' viewing this know, these are new tax credits. It's hard for these guys to be up on the new changes. A lot of them have only been around since the 1940's Sam. So, I don't want to throw anyone under the bus. I know it's hard to keep up with things since the 1940s but at the end of the day you need a specialist to come in. Help get these things done with your person. We don't charge any fee up front.

Jace McDonald:

Take a look with, see what you're eligible for. It's a pretty easy process. We have a team that will follow up with you, but with the sad thing is the dentists, we just got $134,000 back for, Sam, was too busy to return a call for weeks. His wife finally realized that this was not in the process. She had heard us talk about this and I think you were at one of the events we spoke at a few months back and we get a call and the wife says, "Oh my gosh, we really could use this extra money".

Jace McDonald:

Here I was thinking we might get them 10, 20, 30 grand back, again, it's tax free. That's a lot of money getting it back. To see them get $134,000 back and realize they could have had it months earlier. I know for my family it would've been very beneficial to any business getting that, that cash influx. So really the question I have for your members is how soon would they like their money? Let us get them the custom link they need. Get the information rolling in any industry that they're in. If they're paying taxes, they have employees we should be reviewing to see what they're eligible for. Because really with the way the laws are grandfathered, if they don't get their information in, there may be a day where we can only promise one year.

Jace McDonald:

Currently we can go back three years. What a blessing. It's really a blessing.

Sam Frentzas:

Now, does a check get written out to the wife directly.

Jace McDonald:

I'm telling you what, she was mad at her husband and the office staff dragged their feet out in this. And you know, we're finding out that just about nine out of 10 of every one of our reviews we do, we are getting them money. So I'm very confident in that. Also, I'm finding, like you mentioned, the new higher credit. We're also finding at our other companies that about seven or eight out of 10 are eligible. So again, not everyone's getting every single tax credit here, but there are definitely things that are missing out on and to me, I look at it as if you're going to be in business nowadays, take advantage of these credits that were put there to help you stay in business. These credits were put there. I think we hear about a lot on the news how big companies like Amazon and Walmart don't face some of these different taxes.

Jace McDonald:

They're getting these tax incentives. They're getting these tax credits. They're not missing out. And I am finding that around the Midwest, especially, most everyone I talk to, they're missing out on these tax credits. It's very sad.

Sam Frentzas:

What I like about what you're saying is, look, let's see if you're eligible. You're not asking for a dime upfront, which is fantastic. It's government sponsored and you have to be eligible to get them. So it's not, hey, you don't even want any money up front. Which is showing proof of concept, which is what I love of, "Hey, let's see if you're eligible". Then you can talk shop, which has been fantastic.

Jace McDonald:

We've been really blessed, Sam. Sam, we've been blessed not to have to charge a lot of people up front. And because of the volume of the workload, now we're able to do a review, get the initial data all put together so we can come back and let someone know either yes we can help you and the very few no that we can't.

Jace McDonald:

So a majority of these people are and, I want to step back for a second and say my father working for decades for the Wisconsin Public Service Commission, at the PSC, got to see things that most of us just don't get to see. And I want you to think about that for a minute. You know when you can see that there are things out there being missed and you realize you've been missing them for a long time, you don't want to miss out on them anymore. So when we get these credits available, that dentist now, great example, $134,000 back.

Jace McDonald:

Every year, we're going to be able to do the report necessary and documentation necessary so they can start getting those added tax credits. Not only the last three years, but now moving forward. That is an added benefit today that I really want to stress to your members. These are people now that will not have to be missing out on these additional dollars and help their bottom line improve, their bottom line year after year. I think that is another huge benefit for seeing what they've been leaving on the table. Cause Uncle Sam is not calling to say, sorry Sam, you've been missing out on that money. By the way, we're keeping it, by the way. So, that's the difference here. If you're not getting this checked into, you might as well be saying you're thrilled with what you're paying Uncle Sam.

Sam Frentzas:

Nope. So how do I stop phone calls coming to me and start getting everyone over to you and how does, do they get started? How do they see if they're eligible? What would be the best way to get started?

Jace McDonald:

I would say you call a Jennifer and Sara at my office area code (608)-403-7008 real simple (608)-403-7008. We also have a new updated site. They can put information in and recovertaxcredits.com again, that's recovertaxcredits all one word .com and that's just being updated. Now, there are some great videos we have a Senator on there talking about the tax credits for small to mid-sized companies, not just the big boys. We have some wonderful large companies that have taken the time to look at what they're missing, but what I really enjoy more than helping with $200 million type operations, we're helping small mom and pop companies doing anywhere from $250-500,000 to a million and a half. Last week we were across the gamut, all different dollar volumes coming in here. Most of them are under five to $10 million in volume and all of them, I did not see one report last week where we're not getting dollars back for a company, that's exciting. Now I want to mention dollars back, have a comma in there. We're not talking, getting them back 80-90 bucks.

Sam Frentzas:

Right. Now, and what I like about JT, what you're doing is look, let's see if you're eligible, let's see if we're going to go work together and see what you got first. Which, is I think pretty admirable. Most companies and what I've seen out there is give us 1000 bucks and then we'll see you, your late, let's see if we're a fit and if we are, we'll go down that road. If not, Hey, at least you got a chance to look, clear your head, you don't got nothing coming back to you. Or like there're doctors who couldn't believe it. 134 grand and that's pretty that's a nice chunk of change. That's going to be a nice car for that guy's wife. Is she going in there? I promise you.

Jace McDonald:

She said she wished she had it weeks earlier to spend it. And I said, "well we did what we could do". We put the custom link together. We followed up with a call. You know they got busy and I think that's the sad thing. These obstetricians, these dentists, some of the specialty areas of those eye doctors and dentists, contractors that are in specialty areas. Just there's such a unique vast group of HVAC contractors that own heating and air conditioning. They qualify for tax credits that they're not even fully getting the full measure on to benefit them financially. And to all of them, I have one message, how soon would you like your money if we can get you that money in 90 days, a hundred days. I very seldom see these dollars coming over 120 days. So how soon, if they get going on this right now and just thinking a few months, they'd have a tax free check coming to them that maybe they really need it, their company or for their family if they have a kid in college or wants to go to college. Are you funding your retirement enough? Look at what happened just recently.

Jace McDonald:

The markets that had needs dropped. Could you put some of this money in to help your future retirement? I would think so. You know, what do you want to do with the money? Really? That's the question now is how soon do you want the money and what you're going to spend when you get it. But if you don't get this basic information in, to get reviewed, and you put it off, you're missing out on a lot of money coming your way. And again, Uncle Sam is not calling to say you've been missing out on tax credits. How soon do you want your money?

Sam Frentzas:

Well, we're going to make sure that they got the phone numbers, the link, everything that they're going to need to move forward and see if they are. So, look, you've been fantastic. You've worked with a lot of our members and help a lot of them out. This is why we're doing this webinar so I can quit getting beat up with phone calls going, connect me with JT, connecting with JT. Hey, you work with this guy, he worked with that guy. So everybody's going to get it now and we'll see if they're eligible and then you can help more and more people that way. So I want to thank you for taking the time out and coming on this and talking to everybody and we're going to, not only to our members, but we're going to really get this thing out there to let people know, look, this is government sponsored tax credits and if you're eligible, it's tax free.

Jace McDonald:

It is. It's a wonderful blessing. One thing I want you to remember is if there's a better way to do something, would you rather know the first day or the last day? And I really think this is something that when you find out about this on the first day, you need to stop what you're doing. You need to seriously take a look at this. What if you've got money owed to you? You probably do. Most of the people that we're seeing that we're helping, they think they got money owed, they feel they've been paying too much in taxes. I don't know how you feel Sam or your members might feel some of the ones that have called in and probably said they feel like they'd been paying too much. Well, usually if you feel that way, you probably have been, and I don't know if you've ever felt like you're missing out, but the people that aren't getting these credits back, they're missing out.

Jace McDonald:

They know they've been missing out. They felt they were missing out. They felt they had a great professional hired that most of them did and they just, those professionals, I want you to remember, they're not a particular specialist in this area. So all the wonderful tax professionals I've met and CPAs I met none were specialists in this one arena. That's why those business owners have been missing it. No different than if you think about having a car, a basic Chevy or a basic Ford, you're probably not going to go to the European BMW repair shop. You want that specialist in diesel to work on that. So think of that with the taxes. Who's your specialist right now helping you make sure you're getting those credits?

Jace McDonald:

Well, most business owners I talked to, Sam don't have a specialist. They have their basic guy. So this is why they need to call us. And I can't stress it enough. They have their basic guys, they need a specialist, they're overpaying. And Hey, if I'm wrong, it doesn't cost them a penny to have us find out, with our specialists, how much are they owed? And by the way, we don't run across too many that aren't getting anything back. It's very rare and then you can sleep in at night and go, wow, we had this double checked. We know we're not missing out on this. We thought we were. Well, when I really tear into this, usually every company in the Midwest I meet especially, we're finding that just even the simple WOTC credits they're missing out on, and you're correct, Sam, $9,600 up to per new hire. Think about that. Per new hire, that was one employee, that's a big deal. If they're hiring a lot of people all year. And I don't care what industry they're in, if they're going into payroll, they should be getting this.

Sam Frentzas:

Yeah, even if it's one employee, what would you do with that?

Jace McDonald:

So I appreciate it, Sam. I appreciate you helping us get the message out. We enjoy sharing it and so it's a wonderful message. How soon would you like your money?

Sam Frentzas:

Love it. Love it. All right, JT. Look, I want to thank you. And tell the girls their phones are about to go crazy so they can stop calling me and start calling them.

Jace McDonald:

Wonderful. Thanks so much. Have a great day.

www.ingramcontent.com/pod-product-compliance
Lightning Source LLC
Chambersburg PA
CBHW071419210526
45465CB00001B/454